# A Teacher's Journal

# A Teacher's Journal

## *Memories of the Classroom*

**Marilyn S. Hoff**

**Andrews McMeel Publishing**

Kansas City

*A Teacher's Journal*


For information, write Andrews McMeel Publishing, an Andrews McMeel Universal company, 4520 Main Street, Kansas City, Missouri 64111.

02 03 04 05 06 RR2 10 9 8 7 6 5 4 3 2 1

ISBN: 0-7407-2711-7

To the students at
Jonathan Alder High School,
for my wonderful
classroom memories

# Contents

# Acknowledgments

I WOULD LIKE TO THANK everyone who helped me turn this idea into reality. Thanks to my dear friend Patricia Radloff, whose attention to detail saved me numerous rewrites. Thanks to Johanna Conklin for her willingness to share invaluable knowledge about publishing. I want to thank everyone at Andrews McMeel who welcomed my idea. Editor Jean Z. Lucas deserves a special thank-you for her insightful suggestions, patience, and guidance. Thanks to my colleagues Dr. Mark Lorson and Lance Hughes for suggestions and support. And especially to my husband, Ted, whose enduring belief in my abilities, critique of the manuscript, computer assistance, commitment, and love allowed me to fulfill this dream, thank you.

# Introduction

I AM A TEACHER. That defines who I am more than I care to admit. My husband often accuses me of using my "teacher voice" on him, and he's right; I often do. Teaching is the only profession I have and it is the best career I could have ever imagined. There is no other job quite like it. "My kids" are so very important to me. They have given me love, shown their true selves to me, reached out to me, entertained me, kept me young, made me angry at times, disturbed me, and made me glad to be alive and in their presence.

Those of us who teach receive a wonderful gift; we are allowed to work with the future generation. We have a tremendous responsibility but also a wonderful opportunity to influence children. As a high school Spanish teacher, I have taught approximately four thousand students in my twenty-six years in the classroom. Those years have been filled with wonderful, touching, sad, humorous, and difficult experiences. If you are a teacher, you know this is true.

I have found that most teachers wish they had kept a journal preserving all the interesting people and experiences they encountered over the course of their careers; the colleagues who make a difference, the mentors, funny comments students make, and the kids who need nurturing are all part of a teacher's life. The particular students that touch your life, the reasons you became a teacher, the places you taught, your favorite class, and the events that fade with time can be kept in this journal.

How many times have you thought, "Oh, I wish I had written that down. I could write a book"? This journal gives you that opportunity. *A Teacher's Journal* is a means for insightful self-discovery and a tool for personal and professional growth. It can be used by anyone in the teaching field no matter what level or subjects they teach. New teachers will find it an invaluable instructional tool; veteran teachers will be able to use it as a place to recall memories.

It is also a keepsake book. It will enable you, the teacher, to compartmentalize your memories. You can use the book each day as a diary or you can fill in the chapters randomly. Keep it in your classroom for those times when something happens that you don't want to forget.

Each page begins with a thought-provoking question to tap into those memories that are a part of a teacher's life. These are meant to be only guides or suggestions. You don't need to answer every question; choose those that are important to you. There are blank pages at the end to record additional special memories and moments. *A Teacher's Journal* will be something to cherish; a personal history you can pass on to your children and grandchildren. As you recall your teaching memories, look back on your experiences with fondness and reflect on the impact you have made as a teacher.

# Chapter 1

# So, You Want to Teach

Why did you become a teacher? Was there anyone in particular who encouraged your decision?

Did you have a favorite teacher during your school days? What was he or she like?

Can you remember a favorite movie or a television program about teachers that influenced you to become a teacher? What famous teachers have inspired you?

What were your own school days like?

When and where did you graduate from college? What degree did you receive? What career choices were open to you when you graduated from college?

Was a teaching degree required for your first job? What were some of the challenges you faced in obtaining a teaching position?

What was your major and your minor in college? Do these apply to your teaching today?

What were some of your favorite courses in college? Are these pertinent to your teaching today?

Were you required to student teach in college? If so, where did you teach? How did you feel about that experience?

Before you began to student teach, what kind of teacher did you want to be? What, if any, preconceived ideas did you have about teachers, teaching, and students?

Who was your mentor teacher or observing teacher? What did you learn from that person that you did not get in a classroom?

What did you teach as a student teacher, and what were your students like?

What was your worst experience as a student teacher? What was your best experience as a student teacher?

How did your ideas about teaching change after you finished your student teaching?

Which course best prepared you for teaching? What “life experiences” prepared you for teaching?

Do you have a certificate or license to teach? What are you certified to teach?

Do you think it's important to have an advanced degree to be a good teacher? How does it influence your teaching?

## Chapter 2

# How Will I Ever Survive My First Year?

When did you begin teaching? What restrictions did you first encounter as a teacher? How did these affect your expectations of teaching?

What was the name of the school where you had your first teaching job? How big was the school and where was it located?

What subjects did you teach? How many students did you have? What were they like?

What was your beginning salary? What other duties and assignments in your school did you do to earn additional income?

What was your first day of school like? Did you have the first-day jitters?

How did you feel about the responsibility of having your own class?

Did you follow the advice of many veteran teachers, such as "Don't smile for the first three months"? Did it work?

Who was your principal? What was he or she like?

Did you have a mentor teacher to rely on when you needed help, or did another faculty member guide you? What did you learn from that person?

How was your performance evaluated the first year? By the principal, a mentor teacher, or by compiling a portfolio? How did you perform?

Did you have any favorite students? What are these students doing now?

Can you remember what your expectations of students were? Did they do their work, respect you, meet your standards, and comply with your rules? Were your expectations realistic? Were they met?

How did the students treat you as a new teacher?

Did you have a favorite subject or class that you taught? What was it?

As a beginning teacher, how many hours per week did you spend outside of the school day on school-related matters, such as planning, grading, meetings, and parent communications? What responsibility demanded the most attention or time?

What was the most amusing thing that happened during your first year of teaching?

What was the most disturbing thing that happened during your first year of teaching?

How did you feel after finishing your first year of teaching? Did you change your opinion about teaching and students? Were you ready to quit?

What did *you* learn your first year of teaching?

## Chapter 3

# And Now I Am a Veteran

How many years have you taught? What grade level or subjects have you taught?

Why did you choose to teach the particular grade that you do?

What is the biggest challenge you have in dealing with the age group you teach?

What is the most rewarding experience you have encountered with the age group you teach?

Have you ever taught different grades? Which ones? What were some of the differences you noticed between grades? Any similarities?

What is your favorite age group to teach and why?

Do you give letter or number grades? What constitutes an A, B, C, D, or F?

List the schools in which you have taught over the years. Where were these located? Were they public or private, urban or rural?

How do you feel on the first day of school each year? Does the first day get any easier? Are you nervous, excited, or an old pro at handling the kids?

What is a typical school day like for you?

What is your least favorite task when preparing for a new school year?

How much time do you spend on lesson plans each week? How much time do you spend preparing teaching materials? What other teaching responsibilities take up your time during the week?

What is your definition of a "teachable moment"?

What lessons are uniquely your own? Which of these has been the most successful?

Do you use humor in your classroom? Do the students think you are funny? Give an example of how using humor has been successful or unsuccessful in your classroom.

How much money do you spend each year on your classroom and students? What do you buy?

What are some of the physical and emotional changes you have seen students experience? How did you handle these?

What are some of the social or family changes you have seen students experience? How did you handle these?

What matters to you most as a teacher: the students' achievements, the curriculum, the feeling of accomplishment, or something else?

Do you think you are a good role model for your students? Why?

What are some of the trends in education you have experienced? Which of these would you like to see come around again or fade out completely?

What are some of your favorite teaching methods?
How have you had to adapt these methods over the years?

What kind of technology do you use in your classroom? How does it enhance your lessons? How has it changed over the years?

Are there any classes you feel teachers should take to improve their teaching abilities? Which ones?

Do you regularly attend conferences to improve your teaching? If so, what types have you found to be most useful?

Do you belong to any professional organizations? Which ones? How have they helped or influenced your career?

Do you administer district or state tests to your students? What is your opinion of standardized tests? How does standardized testing affect your teaching?

What is one innovation you would like to see in education? Is it possible to achieve this? If so, what is the first step toward accomplishing it?

## Chapter 4

# How Will I Remember All These Names?

Who were some of your best students? What do you remember about them?

Do you have one all-time favorite student? Who and why? What is that student doing now?

Can you remember the total number of students you have taught? How many of their names do you remember? Try to list a few.

Have you encouraged any of your students to pursue teaching as a career? What are these students doing today?

What was the cutest thing a student ever did in class?

What was the stupidest thing a student ever did in class?

What was the weirdest thing you have ever observed a student doing?

What are some of the funny things you remember about a particular student or class?

Name all the class clowns you have encountered in your teaching days.

Can you remember a student who particularly challenged or inspired you? Who was it and how did she or he affect you?

Which students were really motivated and loved learning? How did these students make you feel as their teacher?

List the qualities of an exceptional student.

Did any of your students receive special awards or recognition at the local, state, or national level? Who were the students and what were the awards?

Have you ever received a written or verbal thank-you from a student? What was the reason or occasion?

Who were some of the most difficult students you had in your classes? What do you remember about them?

Do your students use profanity in the hallways, in the classroom, or with each other? How does that make you feel?

Do your students have problems with drugs, alcohol, truancy, smoking, or pregnancy? How do you handle these?

Do you remember one particular child you feel you have helped? Who and how?

List the ways students' behavior has changed toward teachers over the years. Are students more or less respectful, more or less outspoken, more or less sophisticated? Are they more responsive, loving, and eager to confide in you?

What are some of the slang sayings your students commonly have used?

List some of the fads your students have adopted, for example, bobby socks, saddle shoes, body piercing, boys coloring their hair, and girls showing their midriffs.

What kind of music do your students like to listen to? Who are some of the most popular musicians or music groups?

## Chapter 5

# Room 22

Describe your classroom.

What is your favorite thing in your classroom? Why?

Have you ever had to share a room with another teacher? What was this experience like?

Do you use a computer at your desk? Do your students use computers in the classroom? For what purpose?

How does the use of technology impact your teaching and the students?

Do you use Thematic Units in your classroom? Which ones are your favorites?

How do you motivate your students?

What kinds of incentives or rewards do you offer your students for good performances?

Do you read to your students? What books are their favorites?

Do you play games with your students? What games are their favorites?

How would your students rate you as a teacher? What would your students say about your reputation as a teacher? Do they have a nickname for you? Is it positive or negative?

What are some of the daily routines in your classroom?

Do you eat with your students? Why or why not?

How long are your class periods? How is this time divided?

Do you have a Student of the Day or a Student of the Week in your classroom? How is that person chosen?

What is the neatest project your students ever did? What is the messiest? What is the learning task your students enjoy most?

How have you kept your students quiet? Does the same method always work?

Do you believe homework is important? How much homework do you normally give? What kind of assignments?

Describe the best homework assignment you have given.

Describe the dumbest homework assignment you have given that you wish you could take back.

How do your students feel about homework? What was the most outlandish excuse a student has given you for not doing his homework?

Do you have consequences for students who do not do their homework? What are they?

What are the consequences for misbehavior in your room? Missed recess, detention, in-school suspension?

Do you have a "look" when students misbehave or do you have a "teacher voice" that you use? Describe these.

Have you ever caught a student cheating? What happened and how did you handle the situation?

Describe your most embarrassing moment in the classroom.

Do you attend the graduation ceremony in your school district? How does that make you feel?

List what you have learned from your students.

Chapter 6

# What Grade Would You Give These?

List the best and worst principals you have encountered in your teaching career. What were they like?

List the best and worst administrators you have known. What were they like?

List the best and worst administrative decisions you have witnessed.

List the best and worst teachers you have worked with.

List the best and worst workshops or in-services you have attended.

List the best and worst meetings you have attended.

List the best and worst extra duties you have had to perform as a teacher.

List the best and worst committees you have served on.

List the best advice you were ever given about teaching.

List the worst advice you were ever given about teaching.

List the easiest parts of your teaching job.

List the most difficult parts of your teaching job.

What is your favorite school or building in which you have taught? Why?

List the newest and oldest building in which you have taught.

List the best and worst classes you have taught.

List the biggest and smallest classes you have taught.

What is the best time of the year to teach? Why?

What is the worst time of the year to teach? Why?

What is the best day of the week to teach? Why?

What is the worst day of the week to teach? Why?

What is the best time of the day for children to learn? Why?

What is the worst time of the day for children to learn? Why?

What is the best age level to teach? Why?

What is the worst age level to teach? Why?

List your favorite subjects to teach.

List your least favorite subjects to teach.

List your best classroom rules and the ones you never should have tried.

List the best and worst school cafeterias or lunches.

# Chapter 7

# Some of My Best Friends Are Teachers

*(and Administrators)*

Do you remember a particular colleague you turned to for help? Who was it and what was the situation?

What is the ratio of male teachers to female teachers in your school? How does this make you feel?

What is the teachers lounge like in your school?

What are some of the interesting topics of conversation that have been discussed in the teachers lounge?

Do faculty members get together socially? What kind of activities do they do?

Do you ever have to cover other teachers' classes? What is it like being in another teacher's classroom?

Who is the one particular colleague you can confide in and trust? What happy moments do you remember with this person? What sad moments do you remember with this person?

Are the administrators supportive of your teaching? How do they show it?

What is the strangest or funniest topic ever brought up for discussion at a faculty meeting?

What is the most serious topic ever brought up for discussion at a faculty meeting?

List the ideal characteristics of a principal.

Have you ever wanted to be a principal or other school administrator? Why or why not?

If you could, how would you change the way you are evaluated? Do you believe teachers should be given merit pay? Why or why not?

## Chapter 8

# Meet the Parents: Ward and June Cleaver or Al and Peg Bundy?

How does your age compare to the ages of the majority of your students' parents? Does your age make a difference in how they treat you? How?

How many of your students' parents are involved and interested in the education of their children? In what ways are they active?

Are parents supportive of the teachers and the school system? In what ways?

How are parents different today than in the past?

How have the economic conditions of the school district affected how parents feel about education?

Are many of your students' parents divorced? How does that seem to affect the kids?

Have the parents in your school ever honored you? For what reason?

Can you remember any funny notes or conversations with parents? Describe some of these.

Have you ever taught the parents of your students? How does that make you feel?

What are parents most concerned about today? Are they concerned with school safety, how well their kids do on tests, or how new the school buildings are?

Can you remember a difficult situation with a parent, perhaps when you have had to discipline his or her child? What happened?

# Chapter 9

# It Is So Much More Than a Job!

What do you usually wear to school? Is there a dress code you have to follow?

Do you ever have days when you can dress casually? What casual clothing is acceptable in your school?

What is your favorite day of the week? Why?

How do you feel at the end of the school day? How do you feel at the end of each school year?

Are you a coach or an adviser to a club or organization? Why do you choose to do this job?

Do you attend school functions, such as sporting events, dances, proms, fun fairs, PTA meetings, school musicals, plays, and band concerts? What are these like?

Are you required to do these things or do you choose to do them? How does participating in these events make you feel?

Do you have extra duties, such as bus, gym, hall, detention, playground, and recess duty? What are these activities like?

Have you ever been a lead teacher or a department head? What did these jobs entail?

Do you take students on field trips? What is your most memorable field trip experience?

Do you have "snow days" or other weather-related days off? How do you feel on these days? What do you like to do with these extra days off?

There is a saying in education that the best part about teaching is June, July, and August. Is that true for you? What do you do during summer vacation?

How do you feel as summer ends and the school year is about to begin?

Do you remember how you felt when the *Challenger* space shuttle exploded? What reaction did your students have?

How did you feel after the tragedy at Columbine High School? How did the students in your classes react?

Did your school enact any safety measures after school shootings became prevalent? What were they? How did your students react?

When someone asks what you do, are you proud to say, "I am a teacher"? Why or why not?

What kind of teacher did you start out to be and what kind of teacher are you now?

Did you pattern yourself after a teacher you had? In what ways?

What grade would you give yourself? What grade would your students give you?

Have you received any awards for your teaching? What are they?

Have you ever participated in a teachers strike? What happened?

Have you ever wanted to quit teaching and do something else? If so, what?

Have you ever left teaching for a time and then gone back to it? Why? How did you feel when you returned?

# Chapter 10

# Oh, How I Will Miss My Kids!

When do you plan to retire? Why? How many years will you have taught?

Will your district or students honor you when you retire? In what ways?

How do you want to be remembered by your students? Fair, nice, sympathetic, respected, friendly, difficult, or demanding?

Will you miss teaching when you retire? If so, what do you think you will miss the most?

Do you think you will consider returning to the classroom as a substitute teacher? Or will you start another career?

Will you stay in touch with former colleagues and students? Who?

Will you be active in a retired teachers association? How?

The world is full of educators. Do you have a sense that you are part of a large community or fraternity? Do you often meet other teachers when traveling or pursuing other interests? What are some of your experiences?

How has your teaching affected your family? Has being a teacher helped you better relate to your own children?

Would you recommend teaching as a profession? Why?

What advice would you give a new teacher? What are some of the challenges facing teachers today?

If you could live your life over again, would you choose to be a teacher? Why?

List your most important accomplishments as a teacher.

What has made teaching fun for you?

How has teaching touched your life?

# Personal Notes